ULTRATERRANIUM
The Paintings of Bruce Pennington

To my sister and all others who
support the helpless innocent ones.

A CANTICLE FOR LEIBOWITZ
Book cover for Walter M. Miller Jr (Corgi)
1973

ULTRATERRANIUM

The Paintings of Bruce Pennington

Nigel Suckling

Paper Tiger
An imprint of Dragon's World Ltd
Limpsfield
Surrey RH8 0DY
Great Britain

ISBN 1 85028 167 X

EDITOR Michael Downey
DESIGNER Graham Bingham
ART DIRECTOR Dave Allen
EDITORIAL DIRECTOR Pippa Rubinstein

Typeset by Bookworm Typesetting, Manchester, England
Printed in Singapore

The catalogue record for this book is available from the British Library.

OPPOSITE PAGE The Nimbus of the Mercavah
Private work
1968

CONTENTS

INTRODUCTION

Bruce Pennington was born in Somerset in 1944. His career as an artist began early with great encouragement by family and friends, but he was slow in coming to grips with paint. Between the ages of 5 and 9 his pictures were mostly in coloured pencils because these were easier and less messy to use.

'I can well remember the first painting I did at school,' he says. 'It was of a colossal goose composed of a brown globulous head and body with bright vermilion beak and legs. When it was propped up against the wall with all the other children's paintings I was horrified to see the beak had developed a long stream of paint trickling down like a tenuous red serpent. It looked completely ridiculous, so for several years I never ventured into using paints again. At least, not at home where I had a choice.'

Early on he was drawn to the fantastic and produced impossible landscapes peopled with equally impossible creatures, 'wild kingdoms of anarchic beauty'. For a while most of his pictures were in this vein but he did also have some flair for designing conventional houses and furniture.

'Art for me was always an escape route to a different state of existence, and has continued to be a refuge from the everyday tedium that rarely respects or even recognizes the sanctity of beauty in life.'

The two main subjects that appealed to him were opposites linked by the realities in which they existed – the beautiful and the macabre. 'Ordinary' themes, like sport and history, failed to ignite any spark at all in his imagination.

At the age of 9 Pennington underwent a change of interest. Fantasy yielded to a growing passion for drawing birds – creatures that had always held a magical appeal because of their 'ethereal, almost spiritual elusiveness'. For several years they became his main theme and he filled endless sketchbooks with bird drawings, helped by having easy access to the countryside.

This obsession lasted till the age of 15 when other influences gradually took over. 'Conventional teenage interests' he describes them, 'such as films and popular music. Advertising imagery also appealed to me and by then I'd managed to use paints more effectively than in my formative years.'

The only school subject that Pennington did not heartily dislike was art, which he extended with evening classes at the nearby Beckenham College of Art, mostly life drawing with professional models. He was inspired by the college's atmosphere, loving everything about its 'creative cosiness', as he describes it. From then on his every effort was directed towards gaining a place on a full-time course there, and he built up a large stock of drawings and paintings to demonstrate his ability and range. These later helped win him acceptance for an initial two-year course in art and design at Beckenham from September 1960 to July 1962.

'My first impressions were of wonder. Instead of compulsory assembly which began the day at school, there was the warm, congenial haven of a common-room to relax in before classes started. From then on everything was like a dream. Before, at school, the only recreational music we heard was on open days, usually rock and roll, when girlfriends were allowed in to see the military-style exhibitions of that all-male establishment. But in college the music was mellow, traditional jazz or folk, wafting through air scented with

Gauloise cigarettes and turpentine. There was nothing to jangle the nerves or incite violence. Even better, the girls were part of the college, not visitors. I can say without any doubt that for me the '60s started in the totally liberated environment of that place.'

At first his best college works were drawings. He did well in the life and still-life classes, but his pictorial composition tended to be rather rigid and 'unpainterly', concentrating much more on line than colour. Or, as it was then expressed, more Florentine than Venetian.

After a year this all changed because of what Pennington describes as his 'discovery of colour' – literally. 'Before, it had been for me only an arbitrary accessory with little more value than for adding depth or contrast to a picture. Now I learned from the Impressionists about the sheer, intrinsic value of colour and areas of colour – how it needs to be treated with reverence as something magical not mundane.'

For a while the subjects of his pictures became secondary to his interpretation of them in colour. He painted almost anything that came to hand, using everyday scenes as a kind of framework within which to explore various chromatic combinations. The weird landscapes and exotic creatures of his childhood imagination were completely forgotten.

After passing the relevant exams in 1962, Pennington began another two-year course, this time in painting. This coincided with the merger of Beckenham and Bromley art colleges to form the Ravensbourne College of Art sited near Bromley Common. The building, being new, felt rather harsh and austere to begin with but was soon softened by the liberal application of decorative student graffiti to its spotless walls. Looking back on this, Pennington is still mildly surprised by the apparent lack of disapproval from the authorities.

At the new college he took easily to oil paints, delighting in the freedom of choice they offered in terms of opacity, translucence, plasticity and texture. Colour continued to be his main obsession, the subjects varying widely with no evident thread of continuous development. Unlike some really dedicated students, this lack of direction did not really bother him, especially when the others seemed to be growing old before their time, wrestling with such nebulous monsters as 'artistic identity crises' or possibly just through plain overwork.

Then came 1963 and Pennington felt changes in the air: 'Gone were all the nostalgic jazz records and in came rhythm and blues, harmonicas, Mods, Rockers and "permissiveness". In other words, the '60s proper. The building of the Post Office Tower in London seemed to rise concurrently with all that was happening in the country like some giant maypole. All the neuroses and worries that had previously haunted people seemed to evaporate in the climate of the coming era.'

Looking back on the '60s now, Pennington is still astonished by the sudden explosion of 'intelligence' in popular music, art and, in fact, almost every aspect of life. A lingering regret is not having saved enough of the underground posters and magazines that erupted into a startled world. In many ways the period reminds him of the so-called 'decadent' period at the end of the 19th century in which the Symbolist and Art Nouveau movements flowered with artists like Gustave Moreau, Arnold Bocklin, Klimt and Mucha whom Pennington has increasingly come to admire over the years. The *fin de siècle* era remains his favourite in the history of art.

However, one place which seemed immune to the general uplifting of spirits was (in Pennington's eyes, at least) Ravensbourne College of Art. His own vehicles of expression by now were Op and Pop Art, the latter because of its very frivolity which required no profound explanation or motive. 'Life itself was the gift then,' says Pennington, 'as it is now.' But his fellow students seemed to be 'vortexing into gloomy introspection. "Sincerity" was their main objective, being true to their own ideas was all that mattered.

'Of course a government grant made all that easier to believe, but even acceptance and patronage from a top gallery (their ultimate goal) could be unpredictable and precarious if

IMPOSSIBLE POSSIBILITIES
Book cover for Pauwels and Bergier (Mayflower)
1973

they weren't prepared to go along with certain rules of the game, as several naïve artists later found to their cost. Not all gallery owners like their artists suddenly changing their style or subjects, for example, regardless of "sincerity". Also, fashions change and many artists find themselves in clover one year and out in the cold the next.'

Sadly, the sheer pretentiousness of the 'art scene' soured Pennington's last few months at Ravensbourne. The freedom of his early days at Beckenham seemed a far cry from the solemnity which seemed to engulf the students at Ravensbourne as the day of their graduation approached, a solemnity which he did not want to share. His own view was that even if four years at college was enough to warrant some people taking their work and themselves as seriously as seemed expected, he was not one. He knew his own development would be more gradual.

So, determined to 'seek other facets of art itself', he wrote off to several film companies and agencies, prepared to accept anything that offered a challenge. At one point he even applied for work as a make-up artist in a horror film company but their studios were currently out of action. Then a friend from art school rang out of the blue to ask if he was interested in working on film posters.

Pennington rang the small London agency concerned with fairly high interest but was put off by what seemed to him the rather uncompromising tone of the person who replied. He backed off and there it would have ended had he not been prompted later to reconsider and call the number again. This time he accepted the offer of an interview and when he visited the agency he liked the atmosphere very much. They in turn liked his work and signed him on as an illustrator.

'To my art teachers this was the ultimate sell-out, which made me even happier. I relished the sheer vulgarity of the block lettering and orgiastic details of the posters where, it seemed, anything went.'

In a way this work felt like a continuation of his Pop Art phase. In only two months he succeeded in trading 'fine art boredom for commercial art whoredom' and he loved it. Against the background of 'Swinging London' he churned out posters for the agency from September 1964 to July 1966, then he moved briefly to another agency but found the work dull, so a couple of months later he left with the aim of becoming a freelance illustrator.

It proved to be a lean winter, with only a few local commissions to keep him going. However, in the spring of 1967 Pennington's first real commission came from Panther Books who wanted a cover for *The Defence* by Vladimir Nabokov. This led to several other covers for Panther, then in the autumn New English Library (NEL) were impressed enough by his work to commission his first ever science-fiction cover for *Stranger in a Strange Land* by Robert Heinlein. Several other SF novels followed and with this kind of work all Pennington's childhood fascination with the bizarre returned, enriched by his excursions into other fields.

1
SCIENCE FICTION

When Bruce Pennington began producing SF covers for New English Library his basic medium was gouache paint, but to add texture and density he mixed in other materials like polymer paints, tissue paper, inks and varnishes which gave a slightly impasto quality reminiscent of the oils he had used at college. He has continued to use this technique for more or less all his paintings since, certainly all those in this book, mainly because it is much faster than using oil paints.

With NEL he quickly established an easy rapport, which he feels must have contributed to the greater success he enjoyed with these publishers than any other at the time. 'There was never any sense of rigidity or formality,' he says. 'Candour and honesty always prevailed.'

The success of Pennington's early covers soon led to his receiving fan mail. He greatly appreciated this but it did create problems. From the outset he wanted to reply to all the letters but this could be enormously time-consuming, so in practice his responses were erratic. Often he got carried away in his replies and would post off mounds of material with them, but equally often the letters would just lie around gathering dust until they disappeared into that black hole reserved for mail that has been pending too long – something he still feels unhappy about.

The style of Pennington's early SF covers consisted basically of bright colours and a smooth background finish. People often assumed he used an airbrush for his skies and scenery, a notion of which he did not disabuse them in order to guard his professional secrets, but in fact they were achieved by masking off the completed foreground figures with tracing paper and Cow Gum and applying colour washes to the background with very wide brushes. This was often a very tricky process but it appealed to him more than the idea of using an airbrush.

'From the start the very nature of the aerograph, to use its correct name, was alien to me. I did try it on one occasion but my feelings were that it belonged more to the laboratory than the studio. As I uncoiled the cable and set up the compressor I felt part of some hi-tech conspiracy. The illustration, appropriately titled *Satan's World*, was actually quite pleasing but I never used the instrument again for covers. I did occasionally try it later in private works but remained unconverted.'

Pennington's entry into science fiction coincided with the real birth of his interest in mysticism, religion, mythology and, in fact, all aspects of what might broadly be called the paranormal.

Finding the right term to cover this area of interest has often been a problem for Pennington. 'Occult', for instance, often has connotations of black magic and Satanism. 'Supernatural' has associations with spiritualism and ghost-hunting. Resorting to Latin is one way of shedding preconceptions, hence the title of this book: *Ultraterranium* (beyond the world). That, ultimately, is where most of Pennington's interest lies.

In the '60s this led him to an investigation of UFO phenomena which, on reflection, he sees as having much the same elusive appeal for him as ornithology had in his youth. For a while he immersed himself in the theories of W.R. Drake, B.H. Downing, John Michell (*View over Atlantis*, etc.) and others. The subject fascinated him but as time went by he became increasingly disenchanted with many of his fellow enthusiasts.

For instance, in 1970 he went UFO spotting near Warminster where there had been a dramatic sighting about six years before and vigils held ever since. To everyone's delight and wonder a bright orange light duly appeared in the night sky. Was their almost religious awe pricked when someone with binoculars spotted a parachute over the light which meant that it was almost certainly just a military flare? Hardly at all because no one believed him.

This kind of obstinate credulity, common in all the fields of paranormal study, mildly amuses Pennington but for him it reflects only on the people themselves, not the subject of their interest.

During the '70s his investigations moved gradually away from the mechanical to the deeper mystical aspects of the paranormal. Over the years he has grown increasingly certain that the sacred exists as a reality, but in a dimension as yet undiscovered by science: 'It is still, thank goodness, an unviolated realm that continues to inspire me.

'I believe sanctity exists in many forms and locations other than those recognized by orthodox and particularly state religion. Even the most profane music can sometimes contain an instrumental sequence that elevates the average pop song to a level of blissful transcendence. The richness of modern synthetic sounds has a kind of purity I like. Similarly, the most tasteless and gaudy colours used in cheap advertising can occasionally produce an icon of startling beauty. The sacred and symbolic are all around us – only conditioning and low expectations prevent the majority of people from noticing them.'

With popular music he often edits the magical sequences out of the song on to another tape, creating a kind of hymn-like celebration which is all the more wonderful for being completely independent of any recognized religious body.

The Oriental concept of divinity existing as an element within the worshipper appeals to Pennington. 'To most Eastern religions "sin" merely means "error" or mistake from which true seekers of the ultimate truth can learn as they progress. It is never allowed to distract from that goal and any harm done against a seeker is instantly forgiven lest thoughts of vengeance should drag them off course.

The reverse side of an ever-growing interest in things spiritual and sacred is generally a waning of interest in the mundane world, and Pennington is no exception. On the subject of money, for example, he can summon little enthusiasm. While recognizing the necessity of the stuff, he has no interest in it beyond the point of earning a comfortable, even modest, living.

'For me money has no vitality,' he says. 'I cannot find any enthusiasm for it. Occasionally I have considered going into business partnership but I am basically not suited for it. The only true vitality I can see is in people. To make money you need to take it seriously and that can be soul-destructive.'

With good reason, he says, was Pluto, the 'rich one' of Greek mythology (and the root of such words as 'plutocrat'), also the most miserable and ungenerous god of the underworld.

Another consequence of believing in the reality of the sacred is taking on board its shadow side and it was this aspect which noticeably surfaced in Pennington's work as the '70s advanced. Ominous clouds began to encroach upon the clear skies of his early SF paintings and the bright colours darkened. Then, quite abruptly, his imagination and brush entered the realms of horror.

QUEST FOR THE FUTURE
Book cover for A.E. van Vogt (New English Library)
1972

SCIENCE FICTION HALL OF FAME
Anthology cover (Sphere)
1973

LOST WORLD, VOL 1
Anthology cover (Panther)
1973

PREVIOUS PAGE THIRD ASIMOV DOUBLE
Book cover for Isaac Asimov (New English Library)
1973

DECISION AT DOONA
Book cover for Anne McCaffrey (Corgi)
1970

THE CANOPY OF TIME
Book cover for Brian Aldiss (New English Library)
1970

SPACE, TIME AND NATHANIEL
Book cover for Brian Aldiss (New English Library)
1970

EQUATOR
Book cover for Brian Aldiss (New English Library)
1972

THE GREEN BRAIN
Book cover for Frank Herbert (New English Library)
1971

GLORY ROAD
Book cover for Robert Heinlein (New English Library)
1968

BIG SUN OF MERCURY
Book cover for Isaac Asimov (New English Library)
1973

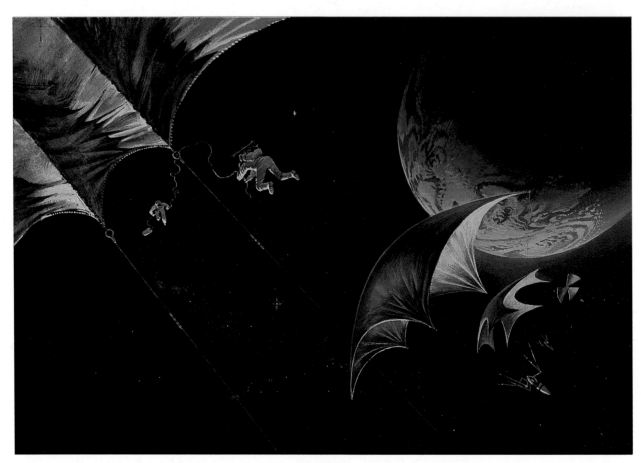

SAILRACE
Cover for A WILDERNESS OF STARS ed. William F. Nolan (Corgi)
1971

INDOCTRINAIRE
Book cover for Christopher Priest (New English Library)
1971

THE MOON IS A HARSH MISTRESS
Book cover for Robert Heinlein (New English Library)
1968

ALIENS FROM SPACE
Book cover for Major Donald E. Keyhoe (Panther)
1974

THE HEAVEN MAKERS
Book cover for Frank Herbert (New English Library)
1974

ON A PLANET ALIEN
Book cover for Barry Malzberg (New English Library)
1975

NEW MAPS OF HELL
Book cover for Kingsley Amis (New English Library)
1968

CHILDREN OF TOMORROW
Book cover for A.E. van Vogt (New English Library)
1972

PIRATES OF THE ASTEROIDS
Book cover for Isaac Asimov (New English Library)
1972

THE MAN IN THE MAZE
Book cover for Robert Silverberg (Star Books)
1981

COMIC INFERNO
Book cover for Brian Aldiss (New English Library)
1973

THE YEAR'S BEST SCIENCE FICTION, NO.6
Anthology cover (Sphere)
1973

A SENSE OF WONDER
Anthology cover for John Wyndham, Jack Williamson and Murray Leinster (New English Library)
1974

NEW WORLDS, No.6
Anthology cover (Sphere)
1973

A Princess of Mars
Book cover for Edgar Rice Burroughs (New English Library)
1968

THE ALIEN WAY
Book cover for Gordon R. Dickson (Corgi)
1971

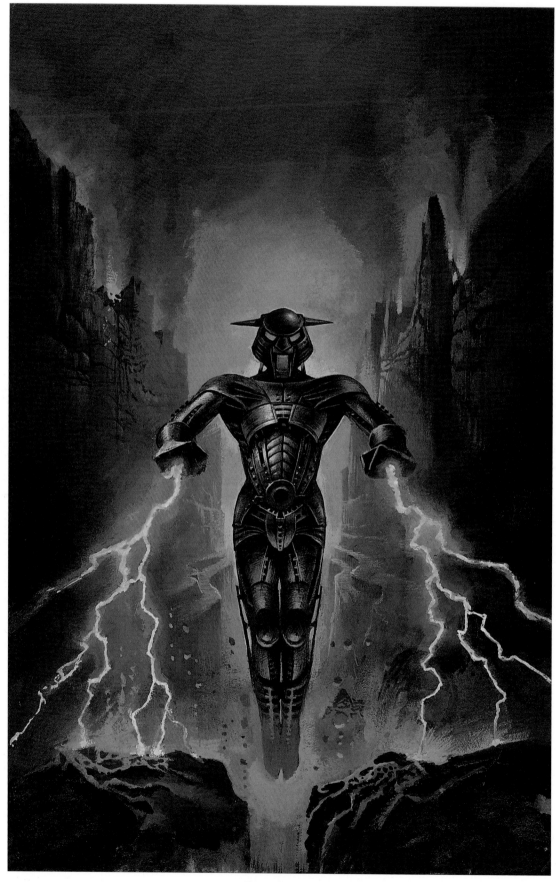

EARTHWORKS
Book cover for Brian Aldiss (New English Library)
1971

SONGMASTER
Book cover for Orson Scott Card (Arrow)
1980

FOLLOWING PAGE LOST WORLDS
Book cover for Clark Ashton Smith (Panther)
1973

2
GOTHIC HORROR

A curious feature of Pennington's career is the way it falls into clearly defined periods with very little overlap. The chapters in this book are in close chronological sequence, as well as grouping his output into distinct categories.

From 1967 to the early '70s Pennington produced almost solely science-fiction paintings. Then, for a while, he produced almost nothing but horror and supernatural covers, and the shift was only marginally due to any personal change of interest. It just happened that SF commissions dried up and horror ones poured in.

This was, he feels, a reflection of the changing mood of the times. Out went the brightly coloured optimism of the '60s and in came a brooding uneasiness about the good intentions of the universe. The change in demand for his brush seemed to parallel the sudden rise of public interest in occultism generally, ranging from the fairly frivolous phenomenon of spoon-bending to the more sinister forms of black magic. The market was suddenly swamped with books and films with the dark side of the supernatural as their theme.

To Pennington it was no coincidence that there was also a sudden increase in moral decay and global pollution. 'It was a distinctly murky, "Neptunian" decade,' he says. 'My paintings became almost monochromatic with a very thick application of paint rarely sharpening into any true detail.'

Many people at the time were surprised by the ease with which Pennington adapted to these darker themes but it was, he says, simply a demonstration of how useful it is to have a firm grasp of style. The mastery of it may be a long and tedious process but in the end it becomes a means of liberation, a chariot of the imagination.

'At art college,' he says, 'I was often criticized for being "too clever" because I could paint or draw in a pastiche or mimicked style of most other artists, but had never really developed one of my own. Worst of all, I had what was most condemned – a technique. Curiously, all students seemed expected to be devoid of the qualities that pre-20th-century artists were applauded for, i.e. a skilful ability to draw and paint any subject accurately.'

Armed with a flexible technique, Pennington left his bright colours on the shelf and applied his brush to the murkier pigments of horror. Did he mind the change?

'Not really. There was a little regret but I would probably have got in a rut without the change. And I always have been almost as interested in the macabre as beauty. I think it is justified to paint something ugly in a beautiful way. After all, nature is a bit like that. Also the Bible states that "The Lord hath made all things for himself, yea, even the wicked for the day of evil." (Proverbs 16:4).

Pennington's most notable covers in the horror genre were commissioned by Panther for two volumes of *Tales of Horror and the Supernatural* by Arthur Machen, the vintage Welsh cult hero. In a way these books were also the first steps on the road to the *Eschatus* project, Pennington's interpretation of Nostrodamus's prophecies, because they helped train his thoughts in that direction. Between them, the two have given rise to a common expectation that Pennington is some kind of gloomy pessimist.

'But the opposite is true,' he says. 'These pictures are not my personal nightmares, just a subject for painting. The mood of *Eschatus* was not my own but Nostrodamus's. Or rather, the mood of his prophecies because he was probably not a gloomy pessimist either. In fact, he led a remarkably interesting life which included finding a secret cure for the plague of his time.'

The violence in many of his pictures from all periods has led to a similar misconception, but he stresses that he has no personal interest in violence other than as a theme for painting. In practice, he is a complete pacifist, to the extent of turning vegetarian in the mid '80s. The main reason was to avoid being party to the ill-treatment of animals, but once he warms to the subject Pennington can quote a good many other arguments in its favour, including physiological evidence that the digestive system of humans is not designed for the consumption of meat. An intended project is a poster filled, rather like a sheet of large postage stamps, with heads of prominent vegetarians, including Buddha, Pythagoras, Socrates, Leonardo da Vinci, Voltaire, Tolstoy, Bernard Shaw, Gandhi and many more.

Apparently, everyone in the Bible was meant to be vegetarian till after the flood, and Pennington firmly believes there is a correlation between the long lifespans of the antediluvian patriarchs and their meat-free diet of 'every herb bearing seed ...' as described in Genesis 1:29. The same meatless diet seemed to extend to all animals as well.

Only with the arrival of the 'Sons of God' did things begin to go wrong, requiring a post-diluvian concession by God that meat could be eaten despite the horrors it would cause (Gen. 9:2–3). 'However, Isiah 2 hints at a time when meat-eating and cruelty will cease, restoring the former age of peace and harmony. And was not Daniel, also a vegetarian, referred to in the Bible as "a man greatly beloved", outshining all his contemporaries in wisdom and honour?'

However, to return to the point, Pennington is a complete pacifist. Painting violence is a form of exorcism and he applies it to many other things which disgust him. He believes it is possible to redeem or neutralize things which are horrible by making them into an aesthetically attractive work, just as Goya in a way redeemed the horrors he saw by showing them to people who otherwise would not have known about them.

There is a therapeutic value in such paintings, he says, as opposed to the way newspapers address the horrors of daily existence, which only makes them banal. In art there is always a battle between ethics and aesthetics, but Pennington believes art can address horror, broadly speaking, in a valuable way that does not require any 'enjoyment' of the theme in the sense of relishing or celebrating it.

Pennington's phase of horror covers ended almost as abruptly as it began when the chance came in late 1975 to concentrate on a private project, the culmination of a growing fascination with and study of prophecy, a branch of the paranormal into which, to this day, he will happily divert any conversation that presents an opening. So far *Eschatus* (1977) is the purest expression of this interest to be published, but it is far from being his last word on the subject, as we shall later see.

TALES OF HORROR AND THE SUPERNATURAL, VOL 1
Book cover for Arthur Machen (Panther)
1974

TWILIGHT
Book cover (Panther)
1974

TALES OF HORROR AND THE SUPERNATURAL, VOL 2
Book cover for Arthur Machen (Panther)
1974

THE ABOMINATIONS OF YONDO
Book cover for Clark Ashton Smith (Panther)
1974

FOLLOWING PAGE BEYOND THE CURTAIN OF DARK
Anthology cover, ed. Peter Haining (New English Library)
1972

TALES OF THE CTHULU MYTHOS, VOL 1
Anthology cover, ed. August Derleth (Panther)
1974

A TIME OF CHANGES
Book cover for Robert Silverberg (Panther)
1974

GHOSTWRITER
Book cover (New English Library)
1975

THE SUNSET WARRIOR
Book cover for Eric van Lustbader (Star Books)
1979

TRAIL OF CTHULU
Book cover for August Derleth (Panther)
1974

THE HORROR HORN
Book cover for E.F. Benson (Panther)
1973

EARTHSHAKER
Calendar illustration (Dragon's World)
1977

3
PROPHETIC VISIONS

The seed of *Eschatus* was sown when Pennington mentioned to Roger Dean of Dragon's Dream that he had a yen to illustrate the Book of Revelation. Nothing immediately came of this and over the next couple of years Pennington discovered Nostrodamus, whose prophecies he decided to illustrate instead. He put the suggestion to New English Library, but while they were considering it, Roger Dean rang to ask if he was still interested in the Revelation project. The timing of this call seemed too neat to be pure coincidence, so, when Dean had no objection to the change of subject, Pennington decided to yield to the nudge of fate and accept the offer, withdrawing his proposal from NEL.

Work on the project took from the autumn of 1975 to the winter of 1976, often at a furious rate as the true scale of the undertaking dawned on Pennington and the necessary deadlines of publishing began to snap at his heels. Often it seemed that the paintings themselves were the least troublesome aspect of the work because he had also undertaken to supply the text. As all existing translations of Nostrodamus's prophecies had to some extent been corrupted by attempts to clarify them, Pennington wanted a fresh translation with as few interpretations as possible. This task meant endless trips to the British Library in London, but to his relief it was later taken over by the editors at Dragon's World (as Dean's company had then restyled itself).

This still left Pennington's written interpretation of the prophecies which, correlated with those in the Book of Revelation, wove an apocalyptic tale of Europe's fortunes from the start of the 22nd century to just before the Great Millennium at the opening of the 24th.

This account started out in the style of the great medieval chronicles, but Pennington was forced to think again because nobody else seemed to appreciate the form. In retrospect he is inclined to agree that the style did not suit the material, robbing it of its mystery without giving anything in return. 'In a way, pictures are better for this sort of thing,' he says. 'Fewer people take offence and no one accuses you of making political points.' However, he was committed to a written interpretation, so, inspired by the example of an old German prophet who produced single-line prophecies for each year, Pennington set about condensing his chronicle into gnomic utterances.

The year or so of *Eschatus*'s production was a period of tremendous strain and sometimes he feels it might have been wiser to wait another ten years or so before tackling it, but the problems were all solved in the end. The book duly appeared on the stands and has remained available ever since.

Given that most students of prophecy seem to interpret the ongoing disasters in the Middle East as proof of imminent Armageddon, why did Pennington set his Great Millennium at the start of the 24th century?

'Because to me all the prophecies of Nostrodamus and Revelation point to an end still centuries in the future. I believe the way news is brought to us distorts our view of the world. All we see and hear about is the small percentage of it which is in trouble, not the greater proportion where everything is fine. The Middle East wars are, of course, dreadful for those involved, but I see no eschatological reason why they should lead to the immediate end of the world. Some people have always read the signs of the end into troubles of their time. Right from the start of Christianity people have understood Revelation to mean that they would see the Day of Judgement in their own lifetimes. Other prophecies get similarly used. There is one of Mother Shipton's going the rounds at the moment predicting the end of the world in 1991. It used to say 1881 but when nothing happened then a new date was found to fit the rhyme.'

As with the subject of UFOs, Pennington does not let himself get carried along with the cranks that a subject like prophecy inevitably attracts. Doing so puts him at odds with many fellow enthusiasts and he has to dismiss much of their evidence and arguments, but enough remains to have convinced him of the reality of the prophetic talent in humans. Nor is this just an academic belief because on a personal level omens are a commonplace reality in his life. The only doubt, as with written prophecies, is when it comes to their correct interpretation.

There is no fixed way of interpreting signs, Pennington says. Uneasiness about seeing black cats or single magpies, for instance, is nonsense. It all depends on the context and timing. A characteristic of omens, it seems, is that what matters is not really the thing in itself but the recognition of it as a sign of something else. In the end omens depend on a human faculty of projecting on to or recognizing in the world signs of what is going on behind the scenes.

Pennington is always looking for patterns, which is part of the attraction of prophecy, astrology and the like. They offer the possibility of stable structures in an otherwise chaotic world which lurches from one calamity to the next because of a lack of any true sense of perspective. The wrong decisions are constantly being made for what seem perfectly sound reasons at the time. Everyone is constantly astonished by how different the world looks in the rear-view mirror. What eschatology (in the broadest sense) offers is a similar perspective on the present and future.

The need or desire for such long-term perspectives is, says Pennington, typical of people with strongly Taurean characters like himself. They like things which are going to last. But need does not necessarily mean suspension of disbelief. As with vegetarianism, Pennington has looked long and hard at the arguments and advocates of the case.

It is difficult to prove that something like astrology is true in a scientific sense because it is (even in its believer's eyes) probably more of an art than a science. Psychological analyses of people's characters and birth charts have shown quite startling parallels, but psychology is not generally recognized as an exact science, so it does not count for much with the sceptics. However, many scientists and mathematicians over the ages have believed in astrology, so it is reasonable to suggest that there is no inherent antagonism between it and scientific reasoning. Their relationship reflects the prejudices of the age.

The principle behind omens is similar to that of astrology in that both claim the existence of connections between things and events which are unrecognized by mechanistic causality. As well as being caused by hidden forces, momentous events send out ripples across time and space. Or, looked at from the opposite angle, 'convergences' as Pennington calls them. The world is full of echoes from the future.

Do any examples of the secret ordering of events come to Pennington's mind? A good one is the American moon-landing in 1969. From an astrological viewpoint, the strength of the Americans' urge to reach the moon first in the '60s was no great surprise because the US national day on 4 July lies in the sign of Cancer, which is ruled by the Moon, so there is a natural affinity. And was it pure coincidence that the landing took place in '69, the astrological sign for Cancer? Or that the actual lunar walk was on a Monday (literally Moon-day) when the Sun (symbol of Apollo, the mission's name) was in Cancer?

The parallels do not end there. Looked back on over a span of twenty-odd years, the '60s as a whole had a decidedly lunar orientation – mysticism, teenage mass hysteria, hallucinogenic drugs, the acceleration of the women's movement. Astrologically it was therefore no great accident that the decade was also a period of US ascendancy and confidence. Such convergences seem to Pennington beyond the bounds of coincidence and worthy at least of consideration.

AQUILA HENRICUS
Illustration for *Eschatus* (Paper Tiger)
1975/6

THE ANTIPOPE
Illustration for *Eschatus* (Paper Tiger)
1975/6

URIEL'S JOURNEY
Illustration for *Eschatus* (Paper Tiger)
1975/6

THE RISE OF ANTICHRIST
Illustration for *Eschatus* (Paper Tiger)
1975/6

THE REIGN OF CARNIVEAU
Illustration for *Eschatus* (Paper Tiger)
1975/6

PREVIOUS PAGE THE NIGHT OF NEMESIS
Illustration for *Eschatus* (Paper Tiger)
1975/6

HENRI'S ERA
Illustration for *Eschatus* (Paper Tiger)
1975/6

REQUIEM
Illustration for *Eschatus* (Paper Tiger)
1975/6

FRATERNAL PACT
Illustration for *Eschatus* (Paper Tiger)
1975/6

4
FANTASY

With the publication of *Eschatus* Pennington turned with relief back to the less demanding and controversial business of book-cover illustration. His publishers had been neglected for two years, but not much ringing around was required before the commissions began rolling in again. This time they came almost solely from the field of fantasy, which again seemed a sign of changing times.

For Pennington it felt very much like a return to his early science-fiction painting, much of which (like his Ray Bradbury covers, for example) was simply fantasy under another label anyway, and it felt like a tremendous release. He still had letters to answer about *Eschatus*, but work transported him to realms of magic castles and the like, where there was nothing portentous or liable to be taken for a serious political or religious point.

Fantasy painting comes so easily to Pennington that often it hardly feels like work. Besides his cover commissions between 1977 and 1985, he produced many pictures for himself for no reason other than that they were decorative and a pleasure to do. Fantasy painting for him is a therapy. He would love to paint a whole wall or room with an endlessly detailed fantasy landscape, but suspects it might be self-indulgent.

The '70s ended in Britain with the 'Winter of Discontent' and almost everyone going on strike. For Pennington this seemed a particularly apt finale. A standard news shot that winter was of mountainous piles of rubbish in black plastic bags, the same kind of bags worn by punk rockers – the youthful face of the decade.

With the '80s a new optimism dawned. It was of a distinctly different kind to that prevailing in the '60s, more self-centred, but nevertheless people seemed to be looking for new ideas and role models. A favourite Pennington preoccupation is characterizing periods by picking out a few salient features, so how would he sum up the '80s?

With 'hard edge' women in business and politics, power dressing with assertive square shoulders, and the craze for women's body building. At the same time there was a wave of effeminate men in pop music and TV. It was almost as if the sexes were trying to become their opposite, seeking an androgynous condition like the alchemists.

'These trends also occurred in the 18th century, "the century of Uranus", when there were similar reversals in the sexes, women taking to wearing masculine clothes and men to using powder and rouge. I would say the '80s were definitely Uranian in character. Uranus itself has its opposite poles equalized, as it were, through its axis being tilted horizontally. It has been dubbed the planet of revolution after its discovery near the time of the French Revolution, and certainly in the USSR and Eastern Europe there was a massive "counter revolution" within a very short space of time in the 80s. The uranium leaks of the time merely reflect the character of the decade.'

For a while in this period fantasy flourished and Pennington was kept as busy with publishing commissions as he could hope for. It felt like a holiday for the artist in him but his curiosity about prophecy was far from satiated.

For Pennington painting and prophecy are more or less equal strands of interest. He feels most fulfilled when they combine and complement each other, but they can and mostly have existed quite independently. This can give rise to conflicting interests. One can have enough of holidays. As the '80s progressed, he felt a growing need for involvement in something serious and by 1985 the demands of his eschatological research had taken over to such an extent that he dropped almost completely out of commercial fantasy illustration, concentrating on private commissions instead.

Does that mean we have seen the last of his work on book covers?

'No, not at all. I am still open to the occasional offer of work and I still sometimes enjoy a good fantasy book. It is just that at the moment other demands on my time seem more important.'

It is fairly certain that the wheel will turn again in due course, perhaps when his current researches reach some culmination and the need for a holiday rises again.

Compared with many, if not most, of his contemporaries in illustration, Pennington has a rugged style. Early on in his film poster days he was impressed by some artists' ability to conjure scenes vividly with just a few bold brushstrokes and has never quite shaken the temptation to do the same. Not that he is entirely comfortable with the habit because he feels that most of his pictures look better when reduced for printing.

He has also sometimes felt a slight isolation when competing for work against illustrators armed with airbrushes and a photo-realistic technique. In the end, however, the style he evolved for book covers was what he was most happy with and he was not interested in changing it drastically for the sake of blending with the competition.

In his private work Pennington often adopts an even sketchier, almost impressionistic style which he personally enjoys, while being aware that it probably has limited public appeal. Some examples of this work can be seen in the final chapter of this book.

What Pennington is more interested in than fine detail is the overall impact of a picture. Although currently involved in other things, book covers and especially posters of all kinds still have an irresistible lure for him because of their powerful imagery.

'An indication of the kind of power imagery can wield occurs sometimes in religious works or political posters which have been known to heal terminally ill people or evoke the most profound patriotism in hardened cynics respectively. Where an artwork scores over literature is in not being restricted by language or cultural barriers, over music in not needing the interpretation of the performer.'

But what exactly is the message being conveyed by fantasy art, especially when detached, as happens in collections like this, from any written story?

The mystery of the unknown, says Pennington. 'The faculty of imagination is what makes people happy. For instance, the stars were more mysterious before everyone knew what they were in a scientific sense. Fantasy art is refreshing in the same way as dreams – it opens the mind to new possibilities.'

BEYOND THIS HORIZON
Book cover for Robert Heinlein (Panther)
1973

THE STONE GOD AWAKENS
Book cover for Philip Jose Farmer (Panther)
1976

FOLLOWING PAGE MUSHROOM LANDSCAPE
Cover for *Asimov Double II* (New English Library)
1972

THE PASTEL CITY
Book cover for M. John Harrison (New English Library)
1971

PREVIOUS PAGE TWO TO CONQUER
Book cover (Arrow)
1982

THE SHADOW OF THE TORTURER
Book cover for Gene Wolfe (Arrow)
1980

ISLAND OF DOCTOR DEATH
Book cover for Gene Wolfe (Arrow)
1981

SHALLOWS OF NIGHT
Book cover for Eric van Lustbader (Star)
1980

RIVERWORLD
Book cover for Philip Jose Farmer (Granada)
1980

THE PAWNS OF NULL-A
Book cover for A.E. van Vogt (Sphere)
1973

GENE WOLFE'S BOOK OF DAYS
Cover illustration (Arrow)
1981

FOLLOWING PAGE DAI-SAN
Book cover for Eric van Lustbader (Star)
1980

FLASHING SWORDS, VOL II
Anthology cover (Granada)
1974

THE CLAW OF THE CONCILIATOR
Book cover for Gene Wolfe (Arrow)
1980

GOTHIC SNOWSCAPE
Private work
1978

PREVIOUS PAGE THE CITADEL OF THE AUTARCH
Book cover for Gene Wolfe (Arrow)
1981

THE BOOK OF FRANK HERBERT
Cover illustration (Granada)
1981

5
ART FOR ART'S SAKE

As Pennington and most other illustrators have discovered, the choice they are faced with at the outset of their career between fine art and illustration as fields within which to exercise their talent is usually an irrevocable one. Unless they can prove the financial viability of an exhibition, illustrators get a chilly reception at most galleries and are made to feel as if they have committed some unpardonable sin. Pennington himself would now only consider exhibiting and selling his work in a gallery if the gallery were his own or of a close friend.

But the curious thing is that most fine artists and illustrators start from the same point – a simple desire to make pictures. However enthusiastically they later embrace the tribal mores of their chosen camp and throw slings and arrows across the divide, the arguments for and against each avenue of expression are rarely self-evident at the outset.

What are those arguments? Well, to summarize them briefly: fine artists mainly accuse illustrators of prostituting their talent for a quick buck; illustrators accuse them of hypocrisy (because in the end the bottom line of any gallery's interest in an artist is whether his/her pictures will sell) and appalling lack of technical skill which they try to obscure with layers of abstract reasoning designed to intimidate the uninitiated.

Given that they start at the same point and have identical ambitions, namely to explore their visual imaginations with the greatest possible freedom, is it not conceivable that the schism between fine artists and illustrators is simply another example of the human genius for creating conflict out of thin air?

It is probably quixotic to suppose that any real resolution of these arguments is possible here, given their deep roots in our culture, but it could be amusing to try.

Suppose, for example, we define a new term, a neutral standard by which both fine artists and illlustrators can be measured. We could call it pure art. Since most members in both camps begin with the same spark of selfless curiosity, we can take that as the standard. Pure art is work which is undertaken purely for its own sake. The degree to which one is a pure artist is measured by the gap between the bulk of the work you produce and that which you would produce if given a year's sabbatical by some rich client, without succumbing to self-indulgence.

Pure artists of the 100 per cent variety are a rare breed. As with any other profession, ideals usually have to be tailored to some extent to suit reality. Some might argue that illustrators by definition cannot be pure artists because they are always working to someone else's text and requirements, but is that necessarily any more constricting than having to meet the demands of public taste in the fine art world? And what do you call it when an illustrator starts painting his or her own ideas for no reason other than selfless curiosity?

The test can be applied equally to fine artist and illustrator. Compare their private work with that which pays the mortgage and you can have a measure of how fulfilled the pure artist in them is.

In Bruce Pennington's case, this chapter gives you a chance to judge for yourself because it contains a selection of pictures produced purely for their own sake. Compared to those shown earlier, do they reveal an imagination strangled by the demands of book publishing?

What fine artists generally fail to realize is that the restraints upon an illustrator can be no greater than, say, being asked to do yet another of those nudes the buyers cannot get enough of when what you really want to paint is a derelict steam engine. With enough ingenuity and patience both demands can, in the end, be satisfied. Books contain such a wealth of images that it is not all that hard to find one which satisfies a personal urge as well as saying something about the story itself. Art directors may have certain expectations, but if they like an artist's style and imagination, there is little reason to interfere. Working within certain constraints can even liberate the imagination by concentrating development in certain areas and suggesting ideas that might not otherwise have occurred.

The only real inhibition Pennington has felt in working for publishers is the time it steals from his other main pursuit. As Ecclesiastes may have said, there is a time for having fun and a time for being serious.

'Prophecy cannot be trivialized. It may not be very tangible at any moment but it is like a channel dug ready for the water of life to flow into. Some things are that inevitable.'

The only problem is working out who and when are being referred to. Pennington believes the ambiguity of Nostrodamus and other prophets was a deliberate ploy to protect themselves and their work from the displeasure of their contemporaries, but his researches have uncovered a consistency between the main sources which allows much clarification. All true prophecy, he believes, taps into the same source.

The demanding nature of research leaves little time for painting, something he often feels guilty about. Reading, both at home and in libraries, takes a vast amount of time, but by way of compensation the material is being distilled into a growing mound of cryptic drawings of, he says, 'a distinctly alchemical nature'. Archetypes are what he is after, but beyond this is not easily drawn because of the incompleteness of the work. Would he say, though, that it is a religious work?

Definitely not. 'To me religion has connotations of dogma and received belief linked with nationalism.' What he is interested in is mythology, a rather different thing, also mathematics, linguistics and philosophy (particularly of the Eastern variety), all of which crop up in these diagrams.

Perhaps not too surprisingly, one of the people he admires most is the psychologist Jung because of his inexhaustible curiosity and enormously open mind. He sees Jung as being in a line with Pythagoras and other classical Greeks, taking in the great figures of the Renaissance, particularly Leonardo da Vinci, for whom science, spirituality and art were not mutually exclusive categories. 'Such people' he says, 'were after the essence of things, not just a scientific explanation of their mechanism.'

Eastern mysticism, particularly Hindu and Chinese, has the same appeal for Pennington. Although granting that sometimes in certain sects it degenerates into empty dogma and fanaticism, generally speaking oriental religion has a syncretistic approach which saves its believers from the boorishness that so often characterizes the way Westerners inflict their ideas on the world. He would love to know what the people of India really thought of the British marching in to take over their country with barely an inkling of what made it tick.

For the future his main objective is to synthesize all the different facets of his work into a single evolved style: 'As yet there are too many diverse interests, as well as painting, which are queueing up to be given some kind of recognition in my pictures; and they are too widely separated to be unified that easily.'

In particular he hopes to distil his mound of 'rather scruffy monochromes' into something more artistic, possibly along the lines of *Eschatus*, but when this will be he has little idea. He just presses on as quickly as circumstances permit.

LAGHIMA
Private work
1986

FUNGUS GIGANTICA
Private work
1990

THE BARLEY TOWER
Private work
1985

BEYOND THE CITY
Private work
1990

SHIVA-SHAKTI
Private work
1986

HELM OF THE CRUCIATIS
Private work
1983

ANGUINOUS TROPHY
Private work
1981

THE ENIGMATIC HARBOUR
Private work
1987

MYRMIDONS
Private work
1985

FOREST TEMPLE
Private work
1985

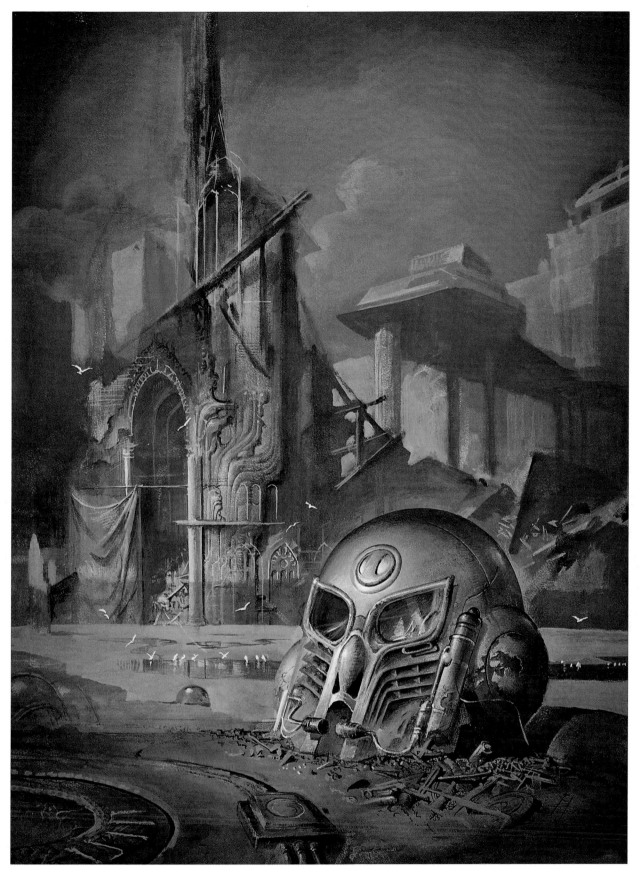

DESERTED ESTUARY
Private work
1988

EASTERN SHORE
Private work
1989

VIEW FROM A TRAIN (APOCALYPTIC DAWNING)
Private work
1973

TEARS FOR A CITY
Private work
1983

EUROPE AFTER ANTICHRIST
Private work
1983

PINK NOCTURNE
Private work
1983

PHOENICIAN TABLEAUX
Private work
1987

AUTUMN OF SILENCE
Private work
1983

NORDIUS
Private work
1985

GATEWAY TO EREBUS
Private work
1984

WINTERSCAPE WITH RUINS
Private work
1983